To Deliciousness
and Beyond

Jenna Miller

Dedication

This book is dedicated to my sweet little boy, my encouraging husband and all my friends and family who always believed in my talents and dreams. *Thank you for all of your continued support and unwavering love.*

A special thank you to our military for their service and for taste testing so many recipes!

Contents

Pecan
Coffee
Cake

Morning Munchies

From classic cinnamon rolls to over-the-top French toast, this chapter of morning munchies will fill you up and satisfy any sweet tooth.

Cinnamon Rolls
with Cream Cheese Icing

SERVES 8

INGREDIENTS

Dough
5 ounces water, heated
   to 105 degrees
   Fahrenheit
4 ounces milk, heated to
   105 degrees
   Fahrenheit
3 Tablespoons
   granulated sugar,
   divided
1 ½ teaspoons active
   dry yeast
1 pound all-purpose
   flour
½ teaspoon kosher salt
2 Tablespoons butter,
   melted

Filling
¾ Tablespoon ground
   cinnamon
¼ cup and 1 Tablespoon
   brown sugar
4 Tablespoons butter,
   melted

Icing
8 ounces cream cheese,
   softened
1 teaspoon vanilla
   extract
1 cup powdered sugar

DIRECTIONS

In a small bowl mix together water, milk, 1 Tablespoon sugar and yeast. Mix and set aside for at least 5 minutes or until the top begins to look foamy.

Meanwhile, in a large bowl mix the remaining 2 Tablespoons of sugar, all of the flour and salt.

Pour the wet ingredients and the melted butter into the dry ingredients and mix together with a rubber spatula.

Once the liquid has been absorbed, place the dough on to a lightly floured surface and knead the dough until it is tight and springs back to the touch.

Place the dough in a large, lightly butter-greased bowl. Cover with a damp dish towel. Allow it to rise in a warm area for 2 hours, or until double the size.

After the dough has risen, lightly grease a deep 8" cake pan. Set aside.

In a small bowl mix together cinnamon, brown sugar and butter. Set aside.

Roll the dough out on a lightly floured surface until it is approximately 11" by 17". Sprinkle the rolled dough with the cinnamon mixture, go all the way to the edges.

Tightly roll up the dough, beginning on the 17" side. With a serrated knife, carefully trim off the edges, if needed, then cut the roll into 8 even pieces.

Place rolls into the prepared pan and allow to rise for about 60 minutes.

Preheat the oven to 350 degrees Fahrenheit. Bake for 40 minutes or until golden and the dough is cooked through.

Make the icing: Whip the cream cheese, vanilla and powdered sugar until smooth. Spread on warm or cooled cinnamon rolls. Store uniced cinnamon rolls at room temperature or iced rolls in the fridge for up to three days.

My husband's passion for Star Wars has rubbed off on me over the years. So much so that when I was invited to a trivia night we decided to have Star Wars as our table theme. I love theming my food appropriately so my cinnamon rolls were a fantastic Princess Leia dessert.

S'more Belgium Waffles

SERVES 8

INGREDIENTS

3 teaspoons active dry
   yeast
¾ cup granulated sugar,
   divided
¾ cup water, heated to
   105 degrees
   Fahrenheit
2 cups honey graham
   cracker crumbs
   (about 12 full sheets)
1 ½ cup all-purpose
   flour
½ teaspoon kosher salt
1 cup milk chocolate
   chips
2 sticks *(8 ounces)*
   butter, melted and
   slightly cooled
2 large eggs, lightly
   beaten
1 teaspoon vanilla
   extract
1 cup marshmallow
   fluff

DIRECTIONS

Add yeast and 2 Tablespoons sugar to the water. Stir until ingredients are mostly dissolved. Set aside for 5 minutes or until the top begins to foam.

Meanwhile, in a large bowl combine remaining sugar, graham cracker crumbs, flour, salt and chocolate chips. Set aside.

In a smaller bowl combine butter, eggs and vanilla.

Pour both the yeast and butter mixtures into the dry ingredients and gently stir the batter with a rubber spatula until the wet ingredients are absorbed and all ingredients are combined.

Cover bowl with a damp towel and allow to rest for 1 hour.

Preheat a Belgium waffle maker to the lowest setting and spray it with non-stick baker's spray.

Measure out a ½ cup of batter and place on one side of the waffle maker. Measure out another ½ cup of batter and place on the other side of the maker. *(Adjust as needed to accommodate your waffle maker.)* Close lid and bake until golden and cooked through. Carefully remove waffles from maker and top each with 2 Tablespoons marshmallow fluff.

Repeat last step until all the batter is used.

One of our tastiest trips was to Belgium.
It was the first time our son had a waffle.
What a high bar to set for all his
future waffle experiences!

Buttermilk Biscuits

SERVES 10

INGREDIENTS

2 ¾ cup all-purpose
flour
1 teaspoon kosher salt
1 teaspoon baking
  powder
3 Tablespoons
granulated sugar
12 Tablespoons cubed
  butter, cold
1 cup buttermilk
1 egg, lightly beaten

DIRECTIONS

Preheat the oven to 350 degrees Fahrenheit. Prepare a baking sheet with parchment paper or a silpat sheet. Set aside.

In a food processor, pulse together the flour, salt, baking powder and sugar.

Place butter in food processor and pulse until butter is broken up and smaller than a corn kernel.

Slowly add the buttermilk while pulsing the dough.

Place dough on floured surface and quickly press it out slightly to create a small rectangle, then fold it over. Roll out the dough until it is roughly 6 inches by 11 inches. Cut dough length-wise to make two long strips then slice each strip into 5 biscuits, making 10 biscuits total. Place a couple of inches apart on prepared baking sheet.

Lightly beat egg and a ½ Tablespoon water together. Brush egg on top and bake for 22 minutes.

Crème Brûlée
French Toast Cake

SERVES 8

INGREDIENTS

8 Tablespoons butter,
    plus extra for
    greasing
½ cup brown sugar,
    lightly packed
5 eggs, lightly beaten
1/3 cup milk
1 teaspoon kosher salt
¼ cup granulated sugar
½ teaspoon ground
    cinnamon
¼ teaspoon nutmeg
7 slices Texas toast

DIRECTIONS

Prepare a 9" diameter, 3 ½" deep round, metal or silicone baking dish by rubbing butter along the inside sides of the dish. Set aside.

In a small saucepan over medium heat, melt the butter then add the brown sugar. Mix until combined then pour onto the bottom of the prepared dish. Set aside.

Gently beat eggs, milk and salt together. Set aside.

In a small bowl mix together the granulated sugar, cinnamon and nutmeg. Set aside.

Carefully place 3 ½ slices of bread onto the bottom of the dish, tearing the bread into smaller pieces to completely cover the butter/sugar mixture.

Pour half of the egg mixture over the first layer of bread.

Sprinkle the cinnamon mixture over the egg mixture.

Place another layer of 3 ½ slices of bread on top of the cinnamon sugar.

Pour the remaining egg mixture over the second layer of bread.

Cover dish with aluminum foil and place in the fridge for at least two hours or overnight.

When you're ready to cook the French toast, preheat the oven to 350 degrees Fahrenheit. If the dish has been in the fridge for only two hours you can place it directly into the oven, leaving it covered with foil. If you let the dish sit in the fridge any longer, allow the dish to sit out at room temperature for 30 – 45 minutes before placing it, foil covered, in the oven. Bake for 45 minutes, covered. Then remove the foil and cook an additional 9 minutes or until the top is golden and puffed up.

Remove from oven. Using a knife, release the bread from the sides of the pan and carefully flip the cake onto another dish for serving. *Be careful not to burn yourself with the hot sugar.* Slice and serve immediately.

Maple Bacon Donuts

INGREDIENTS

Dough
1 cup whole milk,
    heated to 105 degrees
    Fahrenheit
¼ cup active dry yeast
1/3 cup granulated
    sugar, divided
1 egg
1 egg yolk
2 teaspoon vanilla
    extract
3 Tablespoons butter,
    melted
2 ½ cups all-purpose
    flour
1 teaspoon granulated
    salt
Vegetable oil, for frying

Candied Bacon
1 pound thick cut
    bacon
1/3 cup brown sugar

Maple Icing
10 Tablespoons butter,
    room temperature
6 Tablespoons maple
    syrup
1 ¼ - 2 cups powdered
    sugar
Milk, optional

DIRECTIONS

Combine warm milk, yeast and 3 teaspoons sugar. Stir and set aside for at least 5 minutes. You should notice the milk mixture begin foaming.

While the yeast activates, in a small bowl lightly mix together the egg, yolk, vanilla and butter. Set aside.

In a stand mixer bowl with a dough hook attachment, combine flour, salt and remaining sugar. On low speed, add in the egg mixture and yeast mixture. Scrape down sides and bottom as necessary, until the dough forms a ball and bounces back with the touch of a finger.

Allow dough to rest in the refrigerator, covered with a damp cloth for 2 hours.

While the dough rises, prepare the bacon:
Preheat the oven to 400 degrees Fahrenheit. Prepare a deep-sided cookie sheet pan with a metal grate sprayed with cooking spray. Place the bacon in a single layer across the grate. Sprinkle evenly with brown sugar. Bake until crispy, about 20-25 minutes. Allow bacon to cool for a few minutes then move it to a cutting board to cool completely. Once cooled, chop and place in an air tight container in the refrigerator.

Prepare a baking sheet by greasing it with butter. Set aside. Once dough has risen for two hours roll the dough on a floured surface to a 1" thickness. Using a 2 ½" donut cutter, cut out donuts and place on the prepared baking sheet. You can re-roll the scraps as needed doing your best not to overwork the dough as you combine. Cover the donuts loosely with plastic wrap and allow them to rise one hour.

In a deep pot or pan, heat vegetable oil to 360 degrees Fahrenheit. Once heated, carefully place a few donuts into the oil. Allow donuts to cook a few minutes on both sides before allowing them to drain on a paper towel lined pan or plate.

Once donuts are fried, mix icing:
Combine all ingredients until smooth. Add more powdered sugar for more sweetness or stiffer icing. Use milk, if desired, to thin icing.

Assembly your donuts:
1. Ice cooled donuts with maple icing and top with candied bacon.
2. Store assembled donuts in fridge or leave un-iced donuts in an air tight container at room temperature and ice/top when ready to consume.

Apple Strudel

SERVES 4

INGREDIENTS

3 Tablespoons butter
1 Tablespoon all-
  purpose flour
2 honey crisp apples,
  cored, peeled and
  sliced ¼" thick
¼ cup packed brown
  sugar
1/3 teaspoon ground
  cinnamon
1 sheet puff pastry,
  thawed
1 large egg
1 Tablespoon water
¼ cup demerara sugar

DIRECTIONS

Preheat the oven to 425 degrees Fahrenheit.

In a small saucepan over low to medium heat, melt butter. Add flour, apple slices, brown sugar and cinnamon. Stir until combined and cook until apples begin to soften a bit. Remove from heat and set aside. Allow mixture to cool completely.

Place a silpat or parchment paper onto a baking sheet and set aside. Place additional parchment paper on the counter and roll out the puff pastry 1 inch in every direction. Cut down the middle of the center 'panel' of the puff pastry to create two rectangles of the same size. Place one rectangle onto the prepared pan; leaving the other on the counter.

In a small bowl mix together the egg and water. Set aside.

Pour apple mixture down the center of the puff pastry rectangle on the baking sheet. Spread out only slightly leaving plenty of edge along the sides, about 1 ½ inches.

Using a pastry brush, lightly brush some of the egg mixture along the edges of the puff pastry containing the apples. Place the other puff pastry rectangle on top of apples and use a fork to seal the edges.

Lightly brush the top of the strudel with egg wash. Then using a sharp knife slice three slits on top. Then sprinkle on demerara sugar.

Bake for 13 minutes or until puff pastry has risen and is golden.

Serve hot or cold with ice cream or fresh whipped cream. Store in an air tight container in the refrigerator.

Fluffer Nutter Stuffed French Toast
with Caramel Sauce

SERVES 4

INGREDIENTS

Caramel Sauce
½ cup granulated sugar
¼ cup water
1 Tablespoon light corn
  syrup
1/3 cup heavy cream,
  warmed
1 Tablespoon butter
Pinch of kosher salt
½ teaspoon vanilla
  extract

Fluffer Nutter Filling
1 cup marshmallow
  fluff
¾ cup creamy peanut
  butter

French Toast
3 large eggs, lightly
  beaten
¼ cup heavy cream
1 ½ cup milk
3 Tablespoons
  granulated sugar
1 teaspoon vanilla
  extract
½ teaspoon kosher salt
4 Tablespoons butter,
  divided
8 – 1 inch slices soft
  Italian or French
  bread

DIRECTIONS

To make the caramel sauce
In a small saucepan, gently mix the granulated sugar, water and corn syrup until the sugar is dissolved. Clean off the inside of the pot using a pastry brush and a little cold water if you notice any of the mixture has splashed onto the sides *(if the sides are not cleaned the whole batch can crystallize and ruin the caramel).*

Place the pan over medium heat. Do not stir any further. Watching closely, allow the mixture to begin to caramelize. If you notice the center of the sugar becoming darker than the outer ring, gently swirl the sugar - DO NOT STIR. Cook until it reaches a medium-dark amber color. Remove from heat immediately.

Slowly add in the cream while stirring; then add the butter. Stir until well incorporated. Stir in the salt. Allow caramel to cool slightly before stirring in vanilla. Set aside.

To make the fluffer nutter filling
In a small bowl mix the marshmallow fluff and peanut butter until well combined. Set aside.

To make the French toast
In a large, shallow dish whisk together eggs, heavy cream, milk, sugar, vanilla and salt. Set aside.

Place a large sauté pan over medium heat. Melt 2 Tablespoons butter in the pan.

Meanwhile begin dipping 4 slices of bread in the egg mixture, coating both sides. Place the 4 slices into the sauté pan. Brown bread on both sides, remove from saute pan.

Melt 2 more Tablespoons of butter in the sauté pan and repeat previous steps to create 4 more slices of French toast.

Assembly
Place one slice of French toast on a plate and top with about 2 Tablespoons of fluffer nutter filling. Spread gently. Top with another slice of French toast. Drizzle caramel over stuffed French toast. Repeat with remaining 2 slices.

For my first Mother's Day my husband made me a delicious stuffed French toast. What I loved was that he didn't simply follow the recipe, he mixed and matched flavors to make it his own. I was so proud! Ever since, I've loved experimenting with stuffed French toast.

Small-Batch Blueberry Muffins

SERVES 10

INGREDIENTS

Crumble Topping
¼ cup quick oats
¼ Tablespoons all-purpose flour
¼ Tablespoon butter, melted
¼ Tablespoon demerara sugar

Muffin Batter
¾ cup all-purpose flour
1/3 cup whole wheat flour
¾ teaspoon baking powder
½ teaspoon baking soda
1/3 teaspoon granulated salt
½ Tablespoon lemon zest
1 ¼ cup blueberries, divided
1 ½ Tablespoons vegetable oil
1/3 cup granulated sugar
1 eggs, lightly beaten
1 egg yolk, lightly beaten
1 Tablespoon fresh lemon juice
½ teaspoon vanilla extract
½ cup plain Greek yogurt
¼ cup milk

DIRECTIONS

Preheat the oven to 375 degrees Fahrenheit. Prepare a muffin tin with cupcake liners. Set aside.

First prepare the crumble topping by mixing together all of the crumble ingredients. Set aside.

Next prepare the muffin batter. In a small bowl mix together the flours, baking powder, baking soda, salt and lemon zest. Mix with a spoon until combined. Toss in half of the blueberries and stir. Set aside.

In a large bowl lightly beat together the vegetable oil, granulated sugar, egg, egg yolk, lemon juice, vanilla extract, yogurt and milk.

Mix the wet ingredients into the dry ingredients until combined.

Scoop the muffin batter into the prepared cupcake liners and top the muffins with the remaining blueberries then the crumble topping.

Bake for 18-20 minutes or until muffin center is no longer wet-looking and a toothpick comes out clean.

Allow muffins to cool before enjoying.

Apple Pecan Pancake

SERVES 6 - 8

INGREDIENTS

Batter
1 cup all-purpose flour
2 teaspoons baking
  powder
¼ teaspoon salt
¾ cup milk
2 large eggs
½ Tablespoon
  granulated sugar
1 Tablespoon vanilla
  extract

Apples
2 ½ Tablespoons butter
1/3 cup brown sugar
3 Granny Smith Apples,
  cored, peeled and
  sliced into ¼ inch
  wedges
2 teaspoons ground
  cinnamon
1 Tablespoon lemon
  juice
¾ cup pecan pieces

Powdered sugar, if
  desired

DIRECTIONS

Preheat an oven to 350 degrees Fahrenheit.

In a large bowl, mix together the flour, baking powder and salt. Set aside.

In a separate bowl, lightly whisk together the milk, eggs, sugar and vanilla.

Whisk the milk mixture into the dry ingredients. Gently whisk until smooth. Set aside.

In a non-stick 12 or 13 inch saute pan, heat butter and brown sugar over medium heat until melted.

Add in apples, cinnamon and lemon juice. Cook for about 6 to 7 minutes, stirring frequently. The mixture will bubble and thicken. Remove from heat and add in pecan pieces. Evenly spread apples over the bottom of the pan.

Pour the prepared batter over the apples and spread evenly in the skillet and place in preheated oven.

Bake for 20 minutes or until pancake is just cooked through. Don't overbake it or the cake will be dry.

Remove from oven and carefully cut around the edges to loosen, if needed. Quickly flip over pancake onto a serving dish. Slice and top with powdered sugar, if using.

We fell in love with Germany
the moment we drove into it.
The landscapes, the people and
of course the food! This pancake
is inspired by the large German
pancakes that are so delicious!

Pecan Coffee Cake

SERVES 8

INGREDIENTS

Filling
2 Tablespoons all-purpose flour
1 Tablespoon ground cinnamon
¾ cup lightly packed brown sugar
¾ cup chopped pecans
4 Tablespoons butter, melted

Batter
1 stick butter, softened
1 cup lightly packed brown sugar
2 eggs
1 teaspoon vanilla
7 ounces plain Greek yogurt
¾ cup all-purpose flour
¼ teaspoon kosher salt
1 teaspoon baking powder

Toppings
4 ounces cream cheese, softened
1 Tablespoon vanilla Greek yogurt
1 Tablespoon sweetened condensed milk
¼ cup strawberry jelly

DIRECTIONS

Preheat your oven to 350 degrees Fahrenheit. Prepare a traditional, removable bottom angel food cake pan by greasing it with baker's non-stick spray. Set aside.

To make the filling, mix all the filling ingredients together in a small bowl. Set aside.

To make the batter, prepare a stand mixer with a paddle attachment. Beat the butter and brown sugar together until combined and lighter in color.

Add the eggs one at a time, beating well after each addition.

Add the vanilla and plain Greek yogurt. Mix until smooth.

Turn off the mixer and place flour, salt and baking powder on top. Slowly start mixer and blend until just mixed.

Spoon half the batter into a greased angel food cake pan, spread to make an even layer. Evenly sprinkle filling on top of batter. Spoon the rest of the batter on top of filling, making sure the filling is completely covered and the batter is smooth.

Bake 30 minutes or until the toothpick comes out clean. The top will be glossy but set. Allow cake to cool.

While coffee cake is cooling, beat together the cream cheese, vanilla Greek yogurt and sweetened condensed milk until smooth.

Once the cake is mostly cooled, use a knife to loosen the outer edges of the cake from the pan. Lift out the center/bottom piece, exposing the sides of the cake. Now loosen the bottom and center ring of the cake. Flip cake out quickly and carefully onto desired dish.

Top with cream cheese icing and strawberry jam.

Mocha Caramel Milkshake
with Toasted Marshmallows

Sweet Tooth Sips

Who says dessert can't be sipped? From homemade hot chocolate to a milkshake made famous in Chicago, this chapter of sweet tooth sips is sure to put a smile on your face!

Cookies n' Cream Milkshake

SERVES 2

INGREDIENTS

12 cookies & cream
  cookie sandwiches
6 ounces vanilla ice
  cream
¾ cup milk

DIRECTIONS

Place all the ingredients into a blender. Blend until smooth.

It's that easy! This is a great recipe to get the little ones involved!

PB & J Smoothie

SERVES 1

INGREDIENTS

5 ¾ *(about 1 rounded cup)* frozen whole strawberries
½ cup + 1 Tablespoon milk
1 ½ Tablespoons creamy peanut butter
1 ½ teaspoons honey

DIRECTIONS

Place all the ingredients into a blender. Blend until smooth.

Involve the kids with this recipe! Our son loves pushing the blender button.

Mocha Caramel Milkshake
with Toasted Marshmallows

DIRECTIONS

SERVES 1

INGREDIENTS

2 Tablespoons heavy
  cream
4 ounces German
  baker's chocolate,
  finely chopped
3 toasted marshmallows
1/8 cup milk
2 Tablespoons good
  quality caramel sauce,
  plus more for garnish
¼ cup marshmallow
  fluff
9 ounces coffee ice
  cream

In a small microwave-safe bowl, warm cream for a few seconds.

Place chopped chocolate into a small bowl. Pour cream over chocolate and cover with plastic wrap to allow the chocolate to melt. After a few minutes, stir ganache to combine these two ingredients. Heat for a few additional seconds, if needed. Set aside.

On a non-stick baking pan, place three marshmallows and toast under a broiler until golden or your desired toasted-ness. Set aside.

In a blender pour milk, 2 Tablespoons prepared chocolate ganache, 2 Tablespoons caramel sauce and the marshmallow fluff. Top with ice cream. Blend until smooth.

Garnish the glass with extra ganache and caramel sauce. Pour milkshake into the glass and top with toasted marshmallows and additional ganache.

Frozen Hot Chocolate

SERVES 2

INGREDIENTS

Chocolate Ice Cubes
1 ½ cups milk
2 packets *(.71 ounces each)* hot chocolate mix

Whipped Cream
½ cup heavy cream
1 Tablespoons powdered sugar
½ teaspoon vanilla extract

Frozen Hot Chocolate
3 Tablespoons fudge ice cream topping
1 cup milk

Sweetened Cocoa Powder, for garnish

DIRECTIONS

The night before, whisk milk and hot chocolate mix together and pour into an ice cube tray. Freeze overnight.

The following day begin by preparing the whipped cream. In a stand mixer with a whisk attachment, blend heavy cream, powdered sugar and vanilla together until the desired texture. Set aside.

In a blender place fudge topping, milk and prepared chocolate ice cubes. Blend until smooth.

Pour frozen hot chocolate into glasses and top with whipped cream and sweetened cocoa powder.

Going to Las Vegas after turning 21 wasn't about drinking and gambling to me; it was about the food! I fell in love with a frozen hot chocolate there and had to create my own version for when traveling to Vegas wasn't an option.

Salted Caramel Cold Coffee

SERVES 1

INGREDIENTS

Salted Caramel Sauce
1 cup granulated sugar
1 Tablespoon corn
    syrup
¼ cup water
1 cup heavy cream,
    warmed
2 Tablespoons butter
¼ teaspoon kosher
    salt
2 teaspoons vanilla
    extract

Coffee Blend
10 ounces cold coffee
¼ cup heavy cream

Whipped cream, *for
    garnish*
Additional caramel, *for
    garnish*

DIRECTIONS

Salted Caramel Sauce

In a large sauce pan, gently mix the granulated sugar, corn syrup and water until the sugar is dissolved and all ingredients are combined. Brush down the sides of the pan with a pastry brush and cold water if you notice any of the mixture has splashed onto the sides of the pan. Crystals on the side can cause crystallization and ruin the caramel.

Place the pan over medium heat. Do not stir.

Watching closely, allow the mixture to begin to bubble and caramelize. If you notice the center becoming darker than the outer ring, gently swirl the pan – DO NOT STIR. Cook until it reaches a medium-dark amber color. Remove from heat.

Immediately and slowly add in cream, mixing until combined and then add the butter and salt. Stir until well incorporated.

Allow caramel to cool slightly before adding in the vanilla extract. Cool completely. Store in an airtight container in the refrigerator.

Coffee Blend

In a tall glass and using a long spoon, vigorously mix 4 Tablespoons caramel sauce, coffee and heavy cream together.

Top with whipped cream and additional caramel if desired.

Classic Hot Chocolate

SERVES 2

INGREDIENTS

1 cup milk
1 ½ cup heavy cream
1 packet *(.71 ounce)* hot
   chocolate mix
3 ounces baking
   German Chocolate,
   finely chopped
1 teaspoon vanilla
   extract

Optional Toppings
Whipped Cream
Marshmallows
Caramel Sauce
Cocoa Powder

DIRECTIONS

Begin heating milk and cream in a saucepan over medium heat, being careful not to burn the milk.

Once milk has lost its chill and is beginning to warm up, begin whisking in the hot chocolate powder mix.

Once combined, add the chopped chocolate and stir until chocolate is melted.

Remove from heat and add in the vanilla extract.

Serve with whipped cream, marshmallows, caramel sauce or a dusting of cocoa powder!

Chocolate Cake Shake

SERVES 2

INGREDIENTS

24 ounces vanilla bean
   ice cream
½ cup milk
3 chocolate cupcakes
   with chocolate
   frosting *(see page 44)*

DIRECTIONS

Place all the ingredients into a blender and puree until smooth.

If you're from Chicago or you've been there, then you know all about the Chocolate Cake Shake at Portillo's. It's a classic and a must have when we are in town. This recipe uses my cupcake recipe but you could substitute any chocolate cake you may have!

Blueberry Cupcakes with Cream Cheese Frosting

Cupcakes, Brownies & Bars Oh My!

Whether you like a classic chocolate cupcake or a twist on a classic fruit bar, Cupcakes, Brownies & Bars Oh My! is a delicious chapter sure to please.

Dark Chocolate Cupcakes
with Chocolate Buttercream

SERVES 24

INGREDIENT

Cupcakes
1 cup milk
2 Tablespoons coffee
    grounds
2 cups all-purpose flour
2/3 cups natural cocoa
    powder
2 ½ baking soda
1 teaspoon granulated
    salt
1 cup butter, softened
½ cup granulated sugar
2 eggs
1 ¼ teaspoon vanilla
    extract
4 ounces semi-sweet
    baker's chocolate,
    melted and slightly
    cooled
¼ cup mayonnaise

Buttercream
¾ cup butter, softened
4 ounces semi-sweet
    baker's chocolate,
    melted and slightly
    cooled
1 ½ teaspoon vanilla
    extract
2 ¼ cups powdered
    sugar
2 Teaspoons milk

DIRECTIONS

Preheat the oven to 350 degrees Fahrenheit. Line cupcake pans with 24 liners. Set aside.

In a small saucepan heat milk and coffee grounds just until warmed. Remove from heat and allow to steep. Set aside.

Meanwhile in a bowl mix together the flour, cocoa powder, baking soda and salt. Set aside.

In a stand mixer with a paddle attachment, beat the butter and sugar together until the mixture is light in color and slightly fluffy.

On a low speed, add one egg at a time into the stand mixer and blend until incorporated.

Add the vanilla, chocolate and mayonnaise into the stand mixture and blend on low until smooth.

While on low speed, slowly add half of the flour mixture into the stand mixer. Strain out the coffee grounds from the milk *(discard grounds)* and slowly pour the milk into the stand mixer. Then add the final half of the flour.

Divide the batter among the cupcake liners and place in the oven for about 12 – 13 minutes or just until done and a toothpick comes out clean. If you over bake them they will be dry!

While cupcakes are cooling, make the frosting: Beat butter, chocolate and vanilla until smooth. Slowly add in the powdered sugar and 1 Tablespoon milk. Beat until smooth adding the second Tablespoon of milk if frosting is too thick.

Frost cupcakes as desired.

Every child's first birthday is a big deal... for the parents. It was important to me that his cupcakes were perfect. To fit the Star Wars theme, I went with these decedent "Dark Side" cupcakes. He loved them... a lot!

Blueberry Cupcakes
with Cream Cheese Frosting

SERVES 13

INGREDIENT

Blueberry Juice
½ cup frozen
    blueberries
2 Tablespoons water

Cupcakes
1/3 cup butter, softened
1 cup granulated sugar
½ teaspoon vanilla
    extract
1 egg
1 ¼ cup all-purpose
    flour
1 ½ teaspoons baking
    powder
¼ teaspoons granulated
    salt
½ cup milk
¼ cup blueberry juice
¾ cup frozen
    blueberries
1 recipe cream cheese
    frosting (pg 48)

DIRECTIONS

Preheat the oven to 350 degrees Fahrenheit. Place liners in cupcake pans. Set aside.

Make the blueberry juice
In a small saucepan place ½ cup frozen blueberries and water. Heat over low heat until berries are soft and liquid begins to release from the berries. Be careful not to boil or burn them! Place a mesh strainer over a bowl and strain out the juice, gently pressing the liquid out of the berries with a rubber spatula. Set aside.

Make the cupcakes
In a stand mixer, mix together the butter and sugar until well combined and light in color.

Add the vanilla and egg to the butter mixture and beat on low until combined.

In a small bowl mix together the flour, baking powder and salt. In a different bowl mix together the milk and ¼ cup prepared blueberry juice.

With your stand mixer on low, begin slowly adding 1/3 of the flour mixture into the butter. Then add ½ of the milk mixture. Add another third of the flour and the last half of the milk. Finish by adding in the last of the flour. Mix only until incorporated.

Scoop the batter evenly between the cupcake liners. Distribute the frozen blueberries among the cupcakes and place on top *(they will sink slightly as they bake)*.

Place cupcakes in the oven for 25 to 27 minutes or until toothpick comes out clean.

While the cupcakes are baking, make the cream cheese frosting.

When our son turned two we celebrated with a Disney's Frozen themed birthday party; it was his favorite movie after all. He blew out the candle on a blueberry cupcake with cream cheese frosting. What I love about this recipe is that there is no food dye used, all of the color comes from fruit!

Cream Cheese Frosting

FROSTS 13
CUPCAKES

INGREDIENT

8 ounces cream cheese,
  softened
1 ½ teaspoon vanilla
3 cups powdered sugar,
  un-sifted

DIRECTIONS

With a whisk attachment on your stand mixer, whisk the cream cheese for 2 minutes.

Add in the vanilla. Mix until incorporated.

Slowly add the powdered sugar and whip the frosting together for about 2 minutes.

Used finished frosting immediately or place it in an air tight container then place in fridge for a slightly firmer consistency.

Classic Brownies

SERVES 12–15

INGREDIENT

1 ½ cups all-purpose
  flour
½ teaspoon granulated
  salt
¾ cup natural cocoa
  powder
3 large eggs
2 large egg yolks
¼ cup whole milk
1 ½ cups granulated
  sugar
¾ cup brown sugar
1 1/3 cup butter, melted
  and slightly cooled
1 ½ teaspoons vanilla
  extract
4 ½ ounces
  unsweetened baking
  chocolate, melted and
  slightly cooled

DIRECTIONS

Preheat the oven to 350 degrees Fahrenheit. Prepare a 9" x 13" baking pan with non-stick baker's spray. Set aside.

In a small bowl whisk together the flour, salt and cocoa powder. Set aside.

In a large bowl gently whisk together the eggs, yolks, milk and sugars until combined.

Slowly whisk the butter, vanilla and melted chocolate into the egg mixture.

Using a rubber spatula, gently and slowly stir the dry ingredients into the wet mixture. Once combined, pour batter into the prepared baking pan.

Bake for 30 - 35 minutes or until a toothpick comes out clean. Allow brownies to cool completely before cutting. Store in an airtight container.

Orange Cupcakes
with Cream Cheese Frosting

SERVES 12

INGREDIENT

1/3 cup butter,
  softened
1 cup granulated sugar
¼ teaspoon vanilla
  extract
1 egg
2 Tablespoons orange
  zest *(about 2 oranges)*
1 ¼ cup all-purpose
  flour
1 teaspoon baking
  powder
½ teaspoon baking soda
¼ teaspoon granulated
  salt
½ cup fresh orange juice
¼ cup milk
1 recipe cream cheese
frosting (pg 48)

DIRECTIONS

Preheat the oven to 350 degrees Fahrenheit. Place liners in cupcake pans. Set aside.

In a stand mixer, mix together the butter and sugar until well combined and light in color.

Add the vanilla, egg and orange zest to the butter mixture and beat on low until combined.

In a small bowl mix together the flour, baking powder, baking soda and salt.

In a different bowl mix together the orange juice and milk.

With your stand mixer on low, begin slowly adding 1/3 of the flour into the butter. Then add ½ of the milk mixture. Add another third of the flour and then the last half of the milk. Finish by adding in the last of the flour. Mix only until incorporated.

Separate the batter between the 12 cupcake liners.

Place in oven for 20 minutes or until toothpick comes out clean.

While the cupcakes are cooling, make the cream cheese frosting.

For our son's third birthday I needed a
cupcake to fit a Disney's Lion Guard
theme. My first thought was an orange
cupcake because of its color. I used the
same principles in making this cupcake
as I did with the blueberry cupcakes.
I love when recipes can be easily
changed to make a whole new treat!
The cupcakes were a success and
he sure did love them!

Gooey Peanut Butter Blondies

SERVES 12–15

INGREDIENT

2 ¼ cups all-purpose
  flour
½ teaspoon granulated
  salt
1 cup milk chocolate
  chips and peanut
  butter chip mix
3 whole eggs
2 egg yolks
1 teaspoon vanilla
  extract
1/3 cup butter, melted
  and slightly cooled
¼ cup milk
1 ½ cups granulated
  sugar
¾ cup brown sugar
1 cup peanut butter

DIRECTIONS

Preheat the oven to 350 degrees Fahrenheit. Prepare a 9"x13" baking pan with non-stick baking spray. Set aside.

In a large bowl combine the flour, salt and chocolate peanut butter chip mix. Set aside.

Place eggs and yolks in a medium bowl and gently mix. Don't beat air into the eggs, just break the yolks and mix slightly.

Mix vanilla, butter and milk into eggs. Stir in sugars until combined. Then stir in peanut butter.

Pour dry ingredient mix into the wet ingredients and stir together until combined.

Spread mixture evenly into the prepared 9"x13" pan.

Bake 30 - 35 minutes or until top is set. The inside will be super moist and slightly gooey.

Allow to cool completely before slicing. Store in an airtight container.

Caramel Swirl Brownies

SERVES 12–15

INGREDIENT

1 ½ cups all-purpose
flour
½ teaspoon granulated
salt
¾ cup natural cocoa
powder
3 large eggs
2 large egg yolks
¼ cup whole milk
1 ½ cups granulated
sugar
¾ cup brown sugar
1 1/3 cup butter, melted
and slightly cooled
1 ½ teaspoons vanilla
extract
4 ½ ounces
unsweetened baking
chocolate, melted and
slightly cooled
1 cup caramel sauce,
warm (pg 58)

DIRECTIONS

Preheat the oven to 350 degrees Fahrenheit. Prepare a 9" x 13" baking pan with non-stick baker's spray. Set aside.

In a small bowl whisk together the flour, salt and cocoa powder. Set aside.

In a large bowl gently whisk together the eggs, yolks, milk and sugars until combined.

Slowly whisk the butter, vanilla and melted chocolate into the egg mixture.

Using a rubber spatula, gently stir the dry ingredients into the wet ingredients. Once combined, pour batter into the prepared pan and spread evenly.

Pour warm caramel over the brownies and only slightly swirl it into the brownies. The caramel will mostly stay on the top and that's okay!

Bake for 35 to 45 minutes or until a toothpick comes out clean. Allow brownies to cool completely before cutting. Store in an airtight container.

Caramel Sauce

SERVES 12–15

INGREDIENT

1 cup granulated sugar
¼ cup water
1 Tablespoon light corn
   syrup
½ cup heavy cream,
   warmed
3 Tablespoons butter
1 teaspoon vanilla
   extract

DIRECTIONS

In a large sauce pan, carefully mix the granulated sugar, water and corn syrup until the sugar is dissolved. Clean off the inner sides of the pot using a pastry brush and a little cold water, if needed.

Place the pan over medium heat. Do not stir any further.

Watching closely, allow the mixture to begin to caramelize. If you notice the center of the sugar becoming darker than the outer ring, gently swirl the pot - DO NOT STIR. Cook until it reaches a medium-dark amber color. Remove from heat immediately.

Immediately and slowly stir in the cream, then the butter. Stir until well incorporated.

Allow caramel to cool slightly before stirring in vanilla.

*As the caramel cools, it will become thicker. Keep in an airtight container, in the fridge. If you find the caramel to be too thick once chilled, it can be warmed over low heat in a small saucepan.

Chocolate Grenade Bar

INGREDIENT

Base Layer
30 Chocolate sandwich
cookies, filling removed
8 Tablespoons butter,
melted

Mocha Cookie Layer
¾ cup all-purpose flour
1/3 cup natural cocoa
powder
1 ½ Tablespoons instant
coffee powder
1/3 teaspoon baking soda
1/3 teaspoon baking
powder
1/3 teaspoon granulated
salt
4 Tablespoons butter,
room temperature
1/3 cup brown sugar
1/8 cup granulated sugar
1 egg
1 egg yolk
1 teaspoon vanilla extract

Chocolate Fluff Layer
14 ounces Marshmallow
Fluff
¾ cup Semi-Sweet
Chocolate Chips,
melted

Ganache Layer
16 ounces milk chocolate
chips
1 cup heavy cream
12 Chocolate Sandwich
Cookies, Crumbled

DIRECTIONS

Preheat the oven to 350 Fahrenheit. Spray an 8" square baking dish with non-stick baker's spray. Set aside.

First, you'll make the base layer: In a food processor pulse chocolate cookies *(filling removed)* until they are a tiny crumb. Add butter and pulse until butter is absorbed.

Press the cookie crumbs into the bottom of the prepared pan. Use the bottom of a flat drinking glass or measuring cup to make sure the crust is flat and compressed well. Set aside.

Now make the mocha cookie layer: In a small bowl, mix together flour, cocoa powder, instant coffee, baking soda, baking powder and salt. Set aside.

In a stand mixer beat together the butter and sugars until completely incorporated and slightly fluffy.

Slowly add the egg, egg yolk and vanilla extract to the butter mixture. Mix until completely incorporated.

Gradually add the dry ingredients to the wet and mix until everything is incorporated. Scrape the sides of the bowl if necessary.

Add small dollops of cookie dough to the cookie crust layer. Using wet fingers and working carefully, spread the cookie dough until crust is completely covered. Bake for 12 minutes. Allow the first two layers to cool completely.

When cooled, it's time to make the chocolate fluff layer: In a bowl, mix together the marshmallow fluff and melted chocolate until the chocolate is completely incorporated. Scoop mixed fluff into the center of the cooled cookie layer and carefully spread it out to the edges of the pan. Set aside.

Make the ganache: Place chocolate chips in a bowl. Set aside. In a small saucepan heat heavy cream, stirring often, until just before it simmers. Remove from heat and pour over chocolate chips. Do not stir. Cover the bowl and allow it to sit for 3 to 4 minutes before stirring. Once mixed and smooth pour over fluff layer.

Top ganache with crushed chocolate cookie sandwiches. Place in fridge for 3 to 4 hours until set. Slice and serve.

Though this dessert was named by my husband, it was inspired by three dear friends from Illinois. We made a seasonal tradition of visiting a chocolate buffet in Chicago where we enjoyed music, endless chocolate treats and great conversation.

Small-Batch Pineapple Cupcakes
with Pineapple Frosting and Bacon

SERVES 6

INGREDIENT

Cupcake Batter
½ cup canned pineapple chunks, roughly chopped
¼ cup + 1 Tablespoon brown sugar, divided
3 Tablespoons butter, softened
¼ cup granulated sugar
1 egg
¾ cup all-purpose flour
¾ teaspoon baking powder
1/8 teaspoon salt
1/3 cup +2 Tablespoons pineapple juice

Pineapple Buttercream
6 ½ Tablespoons butter, softened
1 ¾ cups powdered sugar
2 – 2 ½ Tablespoons pineapple juice
3 slices crispy apple wood smoked, thick-cut bacon

DIRECTIONS

Preheat the oven to 350 degrees Fahrenheit. Line a cupcake pan with 6 cupcake liners. Set aside.

In a small sauté pan mix chopped pineapple chunks and 1 Tablespoon brown sugar. Place pan over medium heat and sauté for 5 minutes. Remove from heat and set aside.

In a stand mixer on medium speed beat together butter, remaining brown sugar and granulated sugar. Beat until completely combined and smooth.

Add egg to mixer and completely incorporated.

In a small bowl mix flour, baking powder and salt.

With the mixer on low speed, add 1/3 of the flour mix. Allow it to mix a moment before adding half of the pineapple juice. Let the batter come together slightly before repeating: 1/3 dry ingredients and half juice. Finish by mixing in the last of the flour. Mix only until combined.

With a rubber spatula mix in the sautéed pineapple. Scoop batter into the prepared cupcake liners. Place in oven for 15 to 18 minutes until the top of the cupcake springs back at the touch of a finger. Remove from oven.

While cupcakes are cooling, make the frosting: In a stand mixer beat butter until creamy. Slowly mix in 1/3 of the powdered sugar. Mix in pineapple juice and beat on low until incorporated. Mix in remaining powdered sugar. If frosting is too thick, add more juice. If the frosting is too thin, add powdered sugar.

Top cupcakes with a little frosting, less is more! Then top with a large chunk of bacon.

Passion Fruit Tart Bars

INGREDIENT

Crust
4 Tablespoons butter,
  softened
1/3 cup granulated
  sugar
1 egg
1 teaspoon vanilla
  extract
1 cup all-purpose flour
¼ teaspoon baking
  powder
1/8 teaspoon granulated
  salt

Filling
6 egg yolks
3 Tablespoons
  granulated sugar
½ cup all-purpose flour
1 cup passion fruit
  concentrate, thawed
¼ cup water

Powdered Sugar, for
  garnish

DIRECTIONS

Preheat the oven to 325 degrees Fahrenheit. Prepare an 8" x 8" baking dish by spraying it with baker's spray. Set aside.

In a stand mixer fitted with a paddle attachment, beat the butter and sugar, on medium speed, until combined and lightly fluffy.

Add the egg and vanilla to the butter mixture and beat on low until combined.

On low, add the flour, baking powder and salt to the mixer and mix on low just until combined.

Press the dough into the bottom of the prepared baking pan.

Bake for 9 minutes.

While the crust cools, prepare the filling: In a bowl, gently whisk the yolks and granulated sugar until combined. Whisk in the flour, doing your best not to not whisk in too much air.

Using a rubber spatula, stir in the passion fruit and water. Pour fruit mixture over cooled crust.

Bake for about 20 - 22 minutes. You want the top to jiggle just a bit if you wiggle the pan but you don't want it too set or the fruit topping will be chewy.

Allow the pan to cool for 30 - 40 minutes before placing it in the fridge to cool completely. Slice and serve with a dusting of powdered sugar.

*Cinnamon Sugar
Dough Dunkers*

Carb Heaven

••

If you're addicted to bread like I am than this chapter, Carb Heaven, is for you! With recipes ranging from bite-sized treats to yeast-risen breads to sweet, quick-breads, there are a wide variety of recipes for every taste bud.

Cinnamon Sugar Dough Dunkers
with Vanilla Glaze

SERVES 3-4

INGREDIENT

Dough
1 ½ cup water, heated to
   105 degrees
   Fahrenheit
1 teaspoon active dry
   yeast
1 ½ Tablespoons
   granulated sugar
1 ½ cups all-purpose
   flour
½ teaspoons kosher salt
1 Tablespoon vegetable
   oil

Cinnamon Sugar
¾ Tablespoon ground
   cinnamon
½ cup granulated sugar

Vanilla Glaze
2 cups powdered sugar
3 Tablespoons milk
1 teaspoons vanilla
   extract

Vegetable Oil, for
   frying

DIRECTIONS

To make the dough: Combine the water, yeast and granulated sugar. Stir and allow to sit for 5 minutes.

Meanwhile, in a large bowl mix together the flour and salt. Drizzle vegetable oil over top. Then, using a rubber spatula, mix in the foamy, frothy yeast liquid. Mix until all the liquid has been absorbed.

Turn out the dough onto a lightly floured surface and knead until the dough is a ball and the dough "bounces" back after pressing your index finger into it.

Place dough in a lightly oiled bowl and cover with a moist cloth for 2 hours to allow it to rise. It will rise quicker if the room is warm.

Meanwhile, in a wide-mouthed bowl, mix cinnamon and sugar. Set aside.

In another bowl combine the vanilla glaze ingredients and whisk together until smooth. Cover and place in the fridge until you are ready to use.

After your dough has risen to double the size, you can now begin to heat your vegetable oil. In a heavy pot heat your two inches of oil to 360 degrees Fahrenheit.

Using a pair of kitchen scissors, start cutting the dough ball into chunks. Be careful not to deflate the dough too much while doing this. The chunks should be about 2 to 3 inches by 2 inches. This is a rough "chop" so it doesn't have to be perfect!

Fry a few dough dunkers at a time. Once golden brown, immediately place in the cinnamon sugar mixture and coat well. Remove from cinnamon sugar and place on serving dish. Keep frying until dough is gone. Serve with vanilla glaze.

Apple Pie Streusel Bread

INGREDIENT

Topping
8 Tablespoons butter, cold
1/3 cup light brown sugar
2/3 all-purpose flour
1 teaspoon ground cinnamon
¼ teaspoon ground nutmeg

Bread Batter
8 Tablespoons butter, melted
1 cup brown sugar
2 eggs, lightly beaten
21 ounces apple pie filling
1 teaspoon vanilla extract
1 ¾ cups all-purpose flour
2 teaspoons baking powder
¾ teaspoon ground cinnamon
¼ teaspoon granulated salt

DIRECTIONS

Preheat the oven to 350 degrees Fahrenheit. Prepare a 9.25" x 5.25" x 2.75" loaf pan with non-stick baker's spray. Set aside.

Make the topping: Dice cold butter and place it in a bowl. Add the brown sugar, all-purpose flour, cinnamon and the nutmeg. Using your fingers or a food processor, mix ingredients together, breaking down the butter, until it resembles chunky, wet sand. Set aside.

Make the bread batter: In a large bowl mix the melted butter and brown sugar until well combined.

Mix eggs into the sugar mixture and mix until completely combined.

Place apple pie filling into a food processor and pulse two to three times to break down the apples but leaving it in small chunks. Mix pie filling and vanilla into wet ingredients. Set aside.

In a medium sized bowl mix together all-purpose flour, baking powder, cinnamon and salt.

Mix dry ingredients into wet ingredients until combined.

Pour batter into the prepared loaf pan. Top with streusel topping.

Bake for 60 – 65 minutes or until a toothpick poked into the middle comes out clean. Allow loaf to cool before carefully removing it.

Cheesy Pepperoni Bread

SERVES 9

INGREDIENT

16 Tablespoons butter, room temperature, divided
1 cup water, heated to 105 degrees Fahrenheit
2 round Tablespoons active dry yeast
1 Tablespoon granulated sugar
2 ¼ cups all-purpose flour
1 ½ teaspoons kosher salt
½ large yellow onion, diced
3 large garlic cloves, minced
2 cups shredded mozzarella cheese
60 slices pepperoni

DIRECTIONS

Melt 3 Tablespoons of butter and set aside.

Mix water, yeast and sugar together. Set aside for 5 minutes to allow it to foam.

Meanwhile in a bowl, combine flour and salt.

Using a rubber spatula mix the yeast mixture and 3 Tablespoons melted butter into the flour. Once liquid is absorbed, place the dough on a lightly floured surface and knead until the dough forms a ball and springs back.

Place the dough into a lightly vegetable-oiled bowl and cover with a damp cloth. Store in a warm place for about 2 hours or until the dough is about double the size.

While dough rises, prepare the filling: In a small sauté pan, melt 1 Tablespoon butter over medium heat. Add the onion and garlic. Stir for 4 to 5 minutes until the onions are translucent. Remove from heat and set aside.

Prepare a 9.25" x 5.25" x 2.75" bread pan by greasing it with baker's spray. Once the dough has risen, roll it out on a lightly floured surface until its approximately 9 inches by 20 inches.

Spread 8 Tablespoons of soft butter over the entire dough; all the way up to the edges.

Spread the onion mixture evenly over the butter. Top with the cheese and finally the pepperoni.

Roll the dough up, starting at a shortest edge, so that your final loaf is 9 inches in length. Place it in the prepared loaf pan, seam-side down. Allow it to sit for one hour in a warm place.

Begin to preheat your oven to 325 degrees Fahrenheit while the loaf is rising. Once loaf has risen, melt the remaining 4 tablespoons of butter and brush it onto the loaf. Place the loaf in the oven for about 55 minutes or until the internal temperature reaches 190 degrees Fahrenheit. Allow loaf to cool in pan prior to removing and slicing it. Store in fridge and warm up slices as needed. Enjoy within 3 to 4 days.

Living in Italy for almost three years inspired our Friday night tradition of pizza and a movie. But sometimes having pizza during the week is nice too. This bread is perfect for mid-week snacking!

Chocolate Chip Peanut Butter Banana Bread
with Streusel Topping

SERVES 9

INGREDIENT

Streusel Topping
5 Tablespoons all-purpose flour
6 Tablespoons granulated sugar
5 Tablespoons butter, melted
1/3 cup quick oats

Bread Batter
1 2/3 cup all-purpose flour
1 ½ teaspoon baking soda
¾ teaspoon baking powder
¼ teaspoon granulated salt
3 medium bananas, mashed
1/3 cup granulated sugar
½ cup packed brown sugar
½ cup smooth peanut butter
¼ cup plain Greek yogurt
2 eggs, lightly beaten
1 teaspoon vanilla extract
1 cup mini semi-sweet chocolate chips

DIRECTIONS

Preheat the oven to 350 degrees Fahrenheit. Spray a 9.25" x 5.25" x 2.75" loaf pan with baker's spray. Set aside.

First prepare the streusel topping by combining all of the streusel ingredients. Mix and set aside.

Next prepare the bread batter by combining the flour, baking soda, baking powder and salt in a bowl. Set aside.

In a large bowl mix together the bananas, sugars, peanut butter, yogurt, eggs, and vanilla until fairly smooth.

Gently mix the wet ingredients into the dry ingredients. Before they are completely combined, stir in the chocolate chips until well incorporated.

Place batter into the prepared loaf pan. Top bread with streusel.

Bake for 58 – 60 minutes or until the center of the bread is set and a toothpick comes out clean. Allow bread to cool completely in the pan before removing and slicing.

Cheesy Chive Bread

SERVES 6 - 8

INGREDIENT

1 cup water, heated to
  105 degrees
  Fahrenheit
2 teaspoons active
  dry yeast
1 Tablespoon
  granulated sugar
2 ¼ cups all-purpose
  flour
1 ½ teaspoon kosher
  salt
1/2 ounce fresh chives,
  chopped
3 Tablespoons butter,
  melted
4 ounces freshly grated
  medium cheddar
4 ounces freshly grated
  Monterey jack cheese
1 egg

DIRECTIONS

In a small bowl mix water, yeast and sugar together. Set aside for 5 minutes. The yeast will begin to foam.

Meanwhile in a large bowl mix together the flour, salt and chives.

Using a rubber spatula mix the yeast liquid into the flour along with the melted butter. Mix until all the liquid is absorbed.

On a lightly floured surface, begin kneading the dough until it springs back when you press a finger into it.

Grease the large bowl and place the dough back in it. Cover the bowl with a moist towel and store in a warm place for 2 hours.

Grease a 9.25" x 5.25" x 2.75" loaf pan. Set aside.

On a lightly floured surface, roll the dough out to 9" x 12". Evenly spread cheeses over the entire dough surface, even to the edges. Roll up the dough so you create a 9" bread log.

Place bread in the prepared loaf pan, seam-side down and place in a warm area for 2 hours.

Preheat oven to 325 degrees Fahrenheit.

Whisk together the egg and 1 teaspoon of water. Gently brush egg wash onto the top of the bread.

Place loaf pan in the oven for 30 minutes. Remove from oven and allow to cool before removing from pan and slicing.

Lemon Bread

SERVES 10 – 12

INGREDIENT

Bread Batter
4 cups all-purpose flour
3 teaspoons baking soda
¾ teaspoon baking
  powder
1 teaspoon granulated
  salt
5 lemons, zested
1 cup granulated sugar
½ cup vanilla Greek
  yogurt
1/3 cup milk
16 Tablespoons butter,
  melted
¾ cups fresh lemon
  juice
3 eggs, lightly beaten
1 egg yolk

Lemon Icing
1 ½ cup powdered
  sugar
3 Tablespoons fresh
  lemon juice

DIRECTIONS

Preheat the oven to 325 degrees Fahrenheit. Grease a traditional bundt pan. Set aside.

In a large bowl, mix together the flour, baking soda, baking powder, salt, lemon zest and sugar. Make sure to break apart any lemon zest clumps that you may see. Set aside.

In a separate bowl, lightly whisk together the yogurt, milk, butter, lemon juice, eggs and yolk.

Slowly whisk the liquids into the dry ingredients. Mix until combined.

Pour batter into prepared pan and smooth out the top. Place in oven for 40 - 50 minutes. Check doneness with a long toothpick or wooden skewer. Toothpick should come out clean.

Allow loaf to cool slightly before removing from pan.

Once bread is completely cooled whisk together the powdered sugar and lemon juice. Pour over bread.

Pumpkin Cream Cheese Bread

SERVES 6- 8

INGREDIENT

Cream Cheese Mix
16 ounces cream cheese
¼ cup sweetened
    condensed milk
¼ cup milk
1 Tablespoon vanilla
    extract

Batter
15 ounces pumpkin
    puree
½ cup granulated sugar
½ cup brown sugar
16 Tablespoons butter,
    melted
3 eggs, lightly beaten
1 teaspoon vanilla
2 ½ cups all-purpose
    flour
2 teaspoons pumpkin
    pie spice
¾ teaspoon granulated
    salt
2 teaspoons baking soda

DIRECTIONS

Preheat the oven to 350 degrees Fahrenheit. Spray a 9.25" x 5.25" x 2.75" loaf pan with baker's spray. Set aside.

In a stand mixer with a paddle attachment beat together the cream cheese, sweetened condensed milk, milk and vanilla. Blend until smooth. Set aside.

In a large bowl mix together the puree and sugars.

To the puree add the melted butter and mix until well incorporated. Mix in the eggs and vanilla

To that same bowl add the flour, pumpkin pie spice, granulated salt and baking soda. Mix only until combined, don't over mix.

Pour half of the pumpkin bread batter into the loaf pan and spread evenly along the bottom. Top with two-thirds of the cream cheese mixture and spread evenly leaving a little gap around the edges. Using a butter knife or spoon, gently swirl in the cream cheese a bit.

Next top with the remaining pumpkin mixture and smooth it out. Finally, evenly spread the remaining cream cheese. Swirl the cream cheese but this time make sure it is a little more combined with the pumpkin batter. Too much exposed cream cheese can get rubbery in the oven.

Bake for 60 – 63 minutes or until a toothpick comes out clean. Allow to cool before removing it and slicing.

Croque Monsieur Stuffed Pretzels
with a Bechamel Dipping Sauce

SERVES 6

INGREDIENT

Dough

1 ½ cups water, warmed to 110 degrees Fahrenheit

1 ¾ teaspoons active dry yeast

2 teaspoons granulated sugar

3 ½ cups all-purpose flour

2 teaspoons kosher salt

1 ½ teaspoons olive oil

½ cup baking soda

Filling

5 ounces black forest ham

6 ounces gruyere cheese

5 ounces Parmesan cheese, grated

Sauce

2 Tablespoons butter

2 Tablespoons flour

2 cups milk

½ teaspoon kosher salt

DIRECTIONS

In a small bowl mix together the warmed water, yeast and sugar. Mix and set aside.

In a large bowl mix together the flour and salt. Once the yeast has started to foam, add it, along with the olive oil, into the flour and mix together until all the liquid is absorbed.

On a lightly floured surface begin to knead the dough. Continue to do so until the dough becomes a ball and bounces back to the touch.

Place dough into a lightly oiled bowl and cover with a moist towel. Allow the dough to sit in a warm place until doubled in size.

Punch down the dough and knead a few times before placing it back in the bowl, covering it and letting it sit another 30 minutes.

Preheat the oven to 425 degrees Fahrenheit. Prepare two baking sheet pans with either parchment or a silpat sheet.

While dough is rising, place a large stock pot of water on the stove and mix in the baking soda. Heat over medium high heat. Bring water to a boil.

While waiting for the pot to boil, slice the ham and gruyere cheese into thin, long strips. Set aside.

Once the dough has begun to rise again, divide it into 6 equal pieces. Working with one piece at a time with the other dough pieces covered with a moist towel, roll a piece of dough into an 18-inch rope. (*If you find the dough is sticking, add only a little bit of flour to your working surface. The more flour you use the harder it is to roll.*) Then using your fingers and the heal of your hand, lightly press that rope flat to create a 21-inch long flat strip about an inch wide. Fill with 1/6 of the gruyere cheese and ham, spreading out evenly so you get some in every bite. Fold one side of the dough over the ham and cheese and seal it with the other side of the dough to create a stuffed rope. If you find the dough isn't sticking to itself well, add a touch of water to the seam.

Now take your stuffed rope and twist it into a pretzel shape. Press firmly to make sure the dough is stuck to itself so it won't lose its shape while boiling.

Complete the above steps with the other pieces of dough to make a total of 6 filled pretzels.

Continued on next page...

Working with one pretzel at a time, place it in the boiling water for 30 seconds. Remove, allow it to drip off some excess water and place onto a prepared baking sheet. Top generously with Parmesan cheese. Complete the rest of the pretzels.

Bake for 18 – 20 minutes or until the pretzels are golden.

While the pretzels are baking, make the béchamel sauce: In a small saucepan over low to medium heat, melt the butter. Whisk in the flour and cook while constantly whisking for two minutes. Slowly whisk in the milk. Allow the sauce to begin to bubble while still stirring. Once thickened, stir in the kosher salt, adding more to taste if desired.

Baklava-Inspired Bread

SERVES 9

INGREDIENT

Dough
2/3 cup water
2/3 cup milk
¼ cup + ½ Tablespoon granulated sugar, divided
1 Tablespoon active dry yeast
3 ¼ cup all-purpose flour
1 teaspoon kosher salt
¾ teaspoon ground cinnamon, divided
1/8 teaspoon ground nutmeg
8 Tablespoons butter, divided
3 Tablespoons honey

Filling
½ cup pistachios
½ cup walnuts
3 almond biscotti with chocolate on the bottom

Egg Wash
1 egg
1 teaspoon water

DIRECTIONS

Make the dough: Warm water and milk together until they reach 105 degrees Fahrenheit. Add ½ Tablespoon sugar and the yeast to the warmed liquid. Allow this mixture to sit for 5 minutes until it is foamy.

In a large bowl mix together the flour, ¼ cup sugar, salt, ½ teaspoon cinnamon and all of the nutmeg. Pour yeast liquid and 4 Tablespoons melted butter into the bowl with the flour. Mix with a rubber spatula. Once the liquid has been completely combined with the flour, place the dough onto a lightly floured surface and begin to knead the dough until it forms a ball and it bounces back when pressed with your finger. Place dough ball into a buttered bowl and cover with a moist towel for 2 hours.

Making the filling: In a food processor place, pistachios, walnuts, biscotti, and ¼ teaspoon cinnamon. Pulse until it becomes a medium-sized crumb. Set aside.

Mix together 4 Tablespoons melted butter and honey. Set aside.

Grease a 9.25" x 5.25" x 2.75" loaf pan with non-stick baker's spray. Set aside.

On a lightly floured surface roll out the dough to 9" x 16". Spread honey butter over the entire surface. Sprinkle nut mixture evenly over the honey butter. Tightly roll the dough up, starting at the short end, to make a 9" log of bread. Gently place in prepared pan, seam-side down, and allow bread to rise for 1 hour, no cover needed. Preheat the oven to 325 degrees Fahrenheit.

Lightly whisk together one egg and 1 teaspoon water. Brush the top of bread the egg wash. Place in preheated oven and bake for 45 minutes. Once done baking, allow the loaf to cool for 30 minutes before removing from pan. Allow to cool completely before slicing.

A Mediterranean cruise gave us our first real experience with Greek food. From savory to sweet we enjoyed many wonderful treats while at Greek ports; Baklava being one of them. This bread is my way of bringing a little of Greece back home to us.

Cheesecake Ice Cream
with Red Velvet Cookie Pieces
and Graham Cracker Crumb Crust

Chilly Treats

My favorite places we've lived have been warm, coastal areas. So naturally I had to have a Chilly Treats chapter in my cookbook. Most people think of ice cream when they think of warm weather but you'll see a couple of alternatives that are just as delicious.

Key Lime Ice Cream
with Dark Chocolate, Raspberry Jam and Chocolate Covered Graham Crackers

MAKES 1 QT

INGREDIENT

Ice Cream
4 egg yolks
1/3 cup granulated
   sugar
4 Tablespoons
   sweetened condensed
   milk
1 cup whole milk
1 ½ cups heavy cream
1/3 cup fresh key lime
   juice
¼ teaspoon granulated
   salt

Mix-Ins
6 ounces Dark
   Chocolate Sauce
   Topping
6 ounces Seedless
   Raspberry Jam
9 Chocolate Covered
   Graham Crackers,
   roughly chopped

DIRECTIONS

Whisk together yolks, granulated sugar and sweetened condensed milk. Set aside.

In a saucepan over low to medium heat, heat milk and cream until it reaches 150 degrees Fahrenheit. Stir continually to make sure it doesn't burn on the bottom.

Slowly add a half cup of the heated milk mixture to the yolk mixture and whisk quickly.

Now slowly add the yolk mixture into the heated cream while continually stirring.

Keep heating mixture until it reaches 185 degrees Fahrenheit. Remove pan from heat and slowly stir in the key lime juice and salt.

Strain liquid into an air tight container and place in the refrigerator overnight.

Once chilled, begin to churn. While ice cream is churning, place dark chocolate sauce into a piping bag. In a small bowl mix raspberry jam with one teaspoon of water to thin it. Place jam into a separate piping bag.

Once ice cream is a soft-serve consistency, you can begin spooning it into a freezer-safe container, swirling with the dark chocolate, jam and graham crackers as you go.

Place in freezer until firm.

This recipe was inspired by my love of Key Lime Pie. I hadn't tried Key Lime Pie until I was 26 years old. But since my first bite, I've been hooked! If it's on a menu then I'm ordering it!

Chocolate Peanut Butter Pudding Pops

MAKES 6

INGREDIENT

1 box (3.56 ounces)
   chocolate pudding
   mix
2 cups cold milk
2 Tablespoons smooth
   peanut butter

DIRECTIONS

In a large bowl whisk together the pudding mix and milk until smooth.

Warm peanut butter for 30 seconds.

Stir peanut butter into prepared pudding until smooth.

Spoon pudding into popsicle molds. Place sticks or tops, depending on your molds, into the top of the pudding and freeze until solid.

This is a great recipe to make with kids because it's simple to assemble and easy to adjust to your child's taste. If your child can't have peanut butter, try adding mint extract, mini marshmallows or small strawberry pieces. Or substitute peanut butter for a hazelnut spread. Not feeling the chocolate? Try other flavors of puddings!

Peanut Butter Pretzel Pie

MAKES 8

INGREDIENT

Crust
3 level cups pretzel
   sticks
1 stick butter, melted
1 Tablespoon granulated
   sugar

Filling
8 ounces cream cheese,
   softened
½ cup powdered sugar
3 Tablespoons
   sweetened
   condensed
   milk
1 cup smooth peanut
   butter

Caramel Sauce
½ cup granulated sugar
¼ cup water
1 Tablespoon corn
   syrup
1/3 cup heavy cream,
   warmed
1 Tablespoon butter
Pinch of kosher salt
½ teaspoon vanilla
   extract

Strawberry Sauce
¼ cup strawberry jelly
1 Tablespoon water

Whipped Cream
1 ¾ cup heavy cream
½ Tablespoon
   powdered sugar
2 Tablespoons vanilla
   extract

DIRECTIONS

Preheat the oven to 350 degrees Fahrenheit.

Make the crust: In a food processor, place the pretzel sticks, melted butter and sugar. Pulse until the pretzels are a small to medium crumb.

Pour the mixture into a 9" pie pan and firmly press into the bottom and up the sides of the pan.

Bake for 8 minutes. Pull out of oven and cool completely while you mix the filling.

Make the filling: In a stand mixer with a paddle attachment, blend the cream cheese, powdered sugar, sweetened condensed milk and peanut butter until smooth and slightly fluffy. Carefully spread filling onto prepared pie crust.

Cover and place in the fridge while you prepare the sauces and whipped cream.

Make the caramel: In a small saucepan, gently mix the granulated sugar, water and corn syrup until the sugar is dissolved. Clean off the sides of the pot using a pastry brush and a little cold water.

Place the pan over medium heat. Do not stir any further. Watching closely, allow the mixture to begin to caramelize. If you notice the center of the sugar becoming darker than the outer ring, gently swirl the pan - DO NOT STIR. Cook until it reaches a medium-dark amber color. Remove from heat immediately.

Slowly add in the cream then the butter. Stir until well incorporated. Then stir in the salt.

Allow caramel to cool slightly before stirring in vanilla. Set aside to cool further.

Make strawberry sauce: Mix the strawberry jelly and water until smooth. Set aside.

Continued on next page...

Make whipped cream: Whip heavy cream, powdered sugar and vanilla in a stand mixer until it creates stiff peaks.

Spread the whipped cream on top of the pie filling, going all the way to the crust.

Finishing Touches
Top the whipped cream with a drizzle of caramel sauce and strawberry sauce. You can also reserve both sauces and smear some of each on the plate with the pie as it is served.

After having a similar dessert during a trip to Pennsylvania I came home and tried my hand at this sweet, salty, nutty and fruity pie!

Cannoli Ice Cream
with Crushed Cannoli Shells

MAKES 1 1/2 QTS

INGREDIENT

Ice Cream
5 egg yolks
1 cup granulated sugar
½ tsp ground
    cinnamon
1 Tablespoon lemon
    zest
15 ounces ricotta cheese
2 teaspoons vanilla
    extract
2 cups heavy cream
¼ cup milk

Mix-Ins
¼ cup mini semisweet
    chocolate chips
1/3 cup shelled, dry
    roasted with sea salt
    pistachios, coarsely
    chopped
Crushed Cannoli Shells

DIRECTIONS

In a large bowl mix together yolks, sugar, cinnamon, lemon zest, ricotta and vanilla. Set aside.

In a large saucepan over low heat begin heating heavy cream and milk. Once it has reached 150 degrees Fahrenheit, take one cup of the heated liquid and slowly whisk it into the ricotta mixture. Then take the ricotta mixture and slowly whisk it all into the heated cream. Stirring constantly, taking care to scrape the bottom of the saucepan, heat custard until it reaches 185 degrees Fahrenheit. Remove from heat and strain into a food storage container.

Allow custard to sit at room temperature for about 30 minutes. Then cover and place in the fridge overnight.

Pour the cold custard into your ice cream maker and churn until it is a soft-serve consistency. Add in the chocolate chips and pistachios. Churn until incorporated. Place finished ice cream into freezer-safe containers and freeze until firm.

Serve with broken cannoli shells on top.

Cookies & Cream Pudding Pie

SERVES 8

INGREDIENT

27 chocolate cookie sandwiches, divided
6 Tablespoons butter, melted
4 (3.75 ounces each) chocolate pudding cups
2 ½ cups frozen whipped topping, thawed, divided
1 (3.75 ounce) vanilla pudding cup
1 teaspoon vanilla extract

DIRECTIONS

Preheat the oven to 325 degrees Fahrenheit. Prepare a pie pan with non-stick baker's spray. Set aside.

Remove and save the cream filling of 22 cookies and cream cookie sandwiches. *The remaining 5 cookie sandwiches will be used as garnish later.* Set aside filling.

In a food processor, pulse chocolate cookies until they are crumbs. Put the processor on low and add the butter. Place mixture into the pan and firmly press it into the bottom and up the sides. Bake for 6 minutes. Remove from oven and allow it to cool completely.

Place all of the chocolate pudding into a medium-sized bowl. Gently fold in 1 ½ cups whipped topping. Set aside.

In a small bowl fold the remaining whipped topping into the vanilla pudding along with the vanilla extract. Set aside.

Heat the cookies and cream filling, which you reserved earlier, for about 45 seconds, stirring every 15 seconds until it is a liquid. Pour and evenly spread the liquid into the bottom of the pie crust.

Evenly spread 1/3 of the chocolate pudding mixture on the bottom of the crust. Next top it with all of the vanilla pudding mixture, spread evenly. Finally top with remaining chocolate pudding mix and spread to cover the vanilla layer.

Crumble remaining 5 cookie sandwiches by hand and sprinkle on top of the pie.

Cover and freeze the pie for at least 2 hours.

Coffee Ice Cream
with Chocolate Swirls

Serves 1 QT

Ingredient

1 ½ cups heavy cream
1 cup milk
¼ cup medium roast
  coffee grounds
3 egg yolks
¼ cup granulated sugar
½ teaspoon vanilla
  extract
½ - ¾ cup chocolate
  fudge sauce

Directions

Heat heavy cream, milk and coffee grounds until they are 135 degrees Fahrenheit. Remove from heat and let steep for 15 minutes.

Meanwhile beat egg yolks and sugar together. Set aside.

Using a fine mesh strainer, strain out coffee grounds and heat cream mixture until it reaches 150 degrees Fahrenheit stirring consistently.

Slowly whisk 1/2 cup of the heated cream to the yolks. Then slowly whisk the yolk mixture into the cream. Stirring continually, heat until it reached 185 degrees Fahrenheit. Remove from heat and allow it to sit for 20 minutes. Then stir in the vanilla extract.

Strain custard and place mixture into an airtight container and refrigerate overnight.

Once cold, add the mixture to an ice cream maker and churn until it's just past a soft-serve consistency.

Layer the ice cream in a freezer-safe container alternating between ice cream and chocolate fudge sauce. Freeze until firm.

Cheesecake Ice Cream
with Red Velvet Cookie Pieces and Graham Cracker Crust Crumbs

SERVES 1.5 QTS

INGREDIENT

½ cup sugar
3 egg yolks
2 cups heavy cream
2 cups whole milk
1 box (11.1 ounce) Jello
  Brand No-Bake
  Cheesecake Mix
1 teaspoon vanilla
  extract
4 Tablespoons butter,
  melted

½ recipe red velvet
  cookie bars,
  crumbled
  (Recipe pg 120)

DIRECTIONS

Make the ice cream: In a small bowl mix together the sugar and yolks. Set aside.

Place the cream and milk in a saucepan and warm to 150 degrees Fahrenheit. Stir to avoid a film from forming on the top of the milk or bottom of the pan.

Slowly whisk ½ cup heated milk mixture into the eggs. Pour the warmed yolk mixture into the saucepan with the cream and stir to incorporate. Heat mixture until it reaches 185 degrees Fahrenheit, stirring continually.

Remove from heat and strain into a large bowl. Whisk in the vanilla and the "filling" package from the No-Bake Cheesecake box. Place in the fridge overnight.

Make the graham cracker crust mix-in: Begin by heating the oven to 350 degrees Fahrenheit.

Mix the graham cracker crust packet from the No-Bake Cheesecake box with melted butter. On a parchment or Silpat lined baking sheet, press the crumbs into an approximately 8" x 11" rectangle.
Bake for 7 minutes and allow to cool completely.

Make red velvet cookie bars *(see page 120)*. Take half of the completed and cooled recipe and break it up into small chunks. Set aside.

Once the ice cream base is chilled, mix and pour into an ice cream maker until a soft- serve consistency.

In a freezer-safe, air-tight container begin adding the ice cream, cookie crumbles and crust chunks in a swirled manner. The amount you add is really up to you.

Freeze ice cream until firm.

Sugar Cookies

Can't Resist Cookies

Cookies come in all shapes and sizes. In the Can't Resist Cookies chapter you'll find traditional family-favorites and unique new takes on your favorite bite-sized treats.

Double Chocolate Mint Cookies

SERVES 24

INGREDIENT

1 ½ cup all-purpose
  flour
¾ cup unsweetened
  cocoa powder
¾ teaspoon baking soda
¾ teaspoon baking
  powder
¾ teaspoon granulated
  salt
8 Tablespoons butter,
  room temperature
¾ cup brown sugar
1/3 cup granulated
  sugar
1 teaspoon mint
  extract
3 eggs
¼ cup mini semi-
  sweet chocolate chips
¾ cup Andes Mints
  Baking Pieces

DIRECTIONS

In a bowl mix together flour, cocoa powder, baking soda, baking powder and salt. Set aside.

In a stand mixer with a paddle attachment, blend butter and sugars together until slightly fluffy, about 5 minutes.

Add mint extract to butter mixture.

Slowly mix in the eggs, one at a time, scraping after each addition.

On low speed, begin adding the dried ingredients slowly into the butter mixture. Mix until combined.

Add in chocolate chips and Andes Mints pieces. Stir on low, until combined. Do not over mix.

Cover dough and place in fridge for at least 2 hours or overnight.

Preheat the oven to 325 degrees Fahrenheit. Prepare cooking sheet pans with parchment or Silpats.

Scoop 1 ½ inch balls *(for smaller cookies)* or 2 ½ inch balls *(for larger cookies)* placing them 2 inches apart. Lightly press the cookies down to flatten them only slightly.

Bake for 10 – 12 minutes for smaller cookies or 12 – 15 minutes for the larger cookies. The cookies will have cracked slightly on top and no longer look wet. Allow cookies to cool slightly before removing from the baking sheet and onto the cooling rack.

A friend of mine loved these cookies so much she offered to purchase me a one-day ticket to Disney World for the recipe. And as crazy as it sounds, I respectfully declined. Though Disney World is my happy place, I wanted to save this recipe for a cookbook I knew I'd one day write. So Nikki, here's that recipe you wanted!

Oatmeal Cookie and Marshmallow Moon Pies

SERVES 11

INGREDIENT

1 cup all-purpose flour
½ teaspoon baking soda
½ teaspoon salt
1 ½ cup quick cooking
   oats
1 teaspoon ground
   cinnamon
½ teaspoon ground
   nutmeg
4 Tablespoons butter,
   room temperature
¼ cup granulated sugar
¾ cup packed light
   brown sugar
2 eggs
1 ½ teaspoons vanilla
   extract
11 marshmallows

DIRECTIONS

In a medium-sized bowl, mix together flour, baking soda, salt, oats, cinnamon and nutmeg. Set aside.

In a stand mixer with a paddle attachment, blend butter and sugars together until fluffy and pale in color.

With the mixer on low, add one egg at a time to the butter, incorporating well before adding the second egg. Mix in vanilla extract.

Mixing on low, slowly begin adding the dry ingredients into the wet ingredients. Mix only until incorporated.

Cover dough and place in the fridge for at least 2 hours or overnight.

Preheat the oven to 350 degrees Fahrenheit. Prepare cookie sheets with parchment or Silpats.

Remove dough from fridge and scoop in to 1 ½ inch balls. You should get 22 balls. Place them about two inches apart on the cookie sheets.

Bake for 12 minutes. The bottoms will be golden and the overall cookie will be slightly puffy.

Allow cookies to cool on the pan for 2 minutes then carefully flip over half of the cookies. Remove the other half of the cookies and place on a cooling rack. Put one marshmallow on each upside down cookie and place them back in the oven for 2 minutes. Remove pans from oven and top with cooled cookies. Press down gently. Enjoy warm or cooled!

My favorite teacher, and now my dear friend, always made school exciting! Every year she did an outer space unit and she concluded that unit by allowing the kids to build a spaceship and fly to the moon. We have continued this tradition with our son no matter where in the world we live. As a special treat we make our version of a moon pie every year to celebrate.

Cran-Orange Shortbread Cookies

SERVES 16

INGREDIENT

1 ¾ cups all-purpose
   flour
1/4 teaspoon salt
1 Tablespoons orange
   zest
8 Tablespoons butter,
   room temperature
¾ cup granulated sugar
1 large egg
2 ½ Tablespoons fresh
   Cara Cara orange
   juice
¼ cup dried cranberries,
   roughly chopped

DIRECTIONS

In a bowl mix together the flour, salt and orange zest. Break up any lumps of zest you may notice. Set aside.

In a stand mixer with a paddle attachment, blend butter and granulated sugar until well incorporated and fluffy.

On low, add the egg and mix until combined.

Slowly add 1/2 of your dry ingredients. While the flour is still incorporating, slowly add in the orange juice. Before the orange juice is completely absorbed, add the remainder of the flour.

Once the dough is mixed, keep the mixer on low and add in the dried cranberries.

Place dough onto clear plastic wrap and create a 'log' that is about 12 inches long. Wrap tightly in the plastic wrap and place in the fridge overnight.

The next day, preheat the oven to 350 degrees Fahrenheit.

Prepare baking sheets with parchment or Silpats.

Remove the dough from the fridge, unwrap it and slice it into 18 cookies. The easiest way to do this is to cut the log in half. Then cut the two logs in half again, and so on. Place cookies onto the baking sheet, leaving two inches between each cookie. Bake for 15 - 17 minutes or until the bottoms are a deep golden.

"My favorite teacher, and now my dear friend, Sandy always made school exciting! Every year she did an outer space unit and she concluded that unit by allowing the kids to build a spaceship and fly to the moon. We continue this tradition no matter where in the world we live. As a special treat we make our version of a moon pie every year to celebrate."

Very Berry Sugar Cookie Crumble

SERVES 8

INGREDIENT

8 Tablespoons butter, room temperature
1 ¾ cups granulated sugar, divided
1 egg
1 egg yolk
1 Tablespoon vanilla extract
2 cups all-purpose flour
½ teaspoon granulated salt
¼ cup water
3 Tablespoons cornstarch
36 ounces frozen berry mix raspberry, blueberry and blackberry

DIRECTIONS

Preheat the oven to 350 degrees Fahrenheit.

Using a stand mixer with the paddle attachment, beat the butter and 1 ½ cups sugar together until completely incorporated.

On low, mix in the egg, yolk and vanilla until fully incorporated.

Add the flour and salt until the dough comes together. Set dough aside while you make the berry filling.

In a small bowl mix together the water and cornstarch. Set aside.

In a large stove-top pot over medium heat, begin to cook the berries and ¼ cup sugar *(add more sugar to taste if desired)*. Stir occasionally as the fruit thaws. Once bubbly add the cornstarch mixture. Allow it to bubble for 5 minutes on low heat as the liquid thickens. Remove from heat and pour into a 2 ½ quart casserole dish.

Sprinkle small pieces of dough evenly over the berry filling making sure to cover as much of the fruit as you can.

Place dish in oven and bake for 25 – 30 minutes or until the top of the dough begins to brown. Serve hot or cold, on its own or over ice cream!

Chocolate Chip Cookies

SERVES 17

INGREDIENT

1 ¾ cup all-purpose
  flour
½ teaspoon salt
½ teaspoon baking soda
6 Tablespoons butter,
  room temperature
¼ cup granulated sugar
¾ cup light brown
  sugar
2 eggs
1 ½ teaspoon vanilla
  extract
1 ½ cups semi-sweet
  chocolate chips

DIRECTIONS

In a bowl mix together the flour, salt and baking soda. Set aside.

In a stand mixer with a paddle attachment, blend the butter and sugars together until light and fluffy.

With the mixer on low, add one egg at a time; incorporate the egg entirely before adding the next one. Add in the vanilla and mix until smooth.

On low speed, slowly add the dry ingredients into the wet ingredients. Once incorporated, add in the chocolate chips and mix on low until evenly distributed.

Place dough into an airtight container and refrigerate for at least 2 hours or overnight.

Once dough has chilled, preheat the oven to 325 degrees Fahrenheit. Prepare 3 sheet pans with parchment paper or Silpats.

Using a ¼ cup ice cream scoop or measuring cup, create 17 dough balls and distribute them among the prepared sheets pans. Leave room between them as they will spread slightly.

Bake for 20 minutes or until slightly browned on bottom. Once done, allow them to cool for 3-4 minutes before removing them from the baking sheet and onto a cooling rack.

Triple Berry Thumbprint Cookies
with Whipped Goat Cheese Filling

SERVES 21

INGREDIENT

Cookie Dough
8 Tablespoons butter,
    room temperature
½ cup granulated sugar
1 egg
¼ cup triple berry fruit
    spread or jelly
¼ teaspoon lemon juice
1 ½ cup all-purpose
    flour
¼ teaspoon kosher salt

Filling
3 ounces goat cheese log
2 ounces cream cheese,
    softened
2 Tablespoons heavy
    cream

DIRECTIONS

Make the cookie dough: In a stand mixer, blend together the butter and sugar until light and fluffy.

On low, add in the egg. Once almost incorporated add in the fruit spread and lemon juice. Mix until combined.

Add in the flour and salt. Mix until just combined.

Cover and refrigerate dough for 20 minutes.

Preheat oven to 350 degrees Fahrenheit. Prepare two cookie sheet pans with parchment or Silpats.

Scoop and roll about two tablespoons of dough into a ball and place on the cookie sheet. Press your thumb in the middle to create an indentation for the filling. Continue to scoop and indent dough, placing each about 2 inches apart on the baking sheets, until all the dough is used. You will have about 21 cookies.

Bake for 10-12 minutes. Allow cookies to cool completely before filling.

Make filling: Beat together goat cheese, cream cheese and heavy cream until smooth. Pipe desired amount into cooled cookies.

Serving Suggestion
If you are making these cookies to serve immediately, follow directions as stated above and refrigerate leftovers. If you are making these ahead of time, make the cookies and allow them to cool and place into an airtight container. Then just before serving, make the filling and pipe into cookies. Again, refrigerate any leftovers if filled with goat cheese.

Goat cheese on a berry flavored
cookie sounds weird, I know.
But it was inspired by my love of
goat cheese and jam on a cracker.
This dense cookie is definitely
unique and a perfect little sweet
after devouring a meat
and cheese board.

Sugar Cookies

SERVES 12

INGREDIENT

1 ¼ cups all-purpose
   flour
½ teaspoon salt
½ teaspoon baking soda
1 teaspoon cream of
   tartar
8 Tablespoons butter,
   room temperature
1 cup granulated sugar
1 egg
¾ teaspoon vanilla
   extract
¼ cup colorful
   sprinkles, optional

DIRECTIONS

In a bowl mix together the flour, salt, baking soda and cream of tartar. Set aside.

In a stand mixer with a paddle attachment, blend the butter and sugar together until light and fluffy.

Add in the egg and vanilla. Mix until incorporated.

With the mixer on low, slowly add the dry ingredients into the mixer. As the last bit of flour is added, add in the sprinkles, if using. Once dough is mixed, place it in an airtight container and refrigerate for at least 2 hours or overnight.

Preheat the oven to 325 degrees Fahrenheit. Prepare two cookie sheet pans with parchment paper or Silpats.

Create 12 dough balls by scooping about 3 Tablespoons of dough per cookie. Place them on the two prepared sheet pans. Give them plenty of room as they will spread out.

Bake for 18-20 minutes. Once done, allow them to cool for 5-7 minutes on the sheet pan before moving to a cooling rack.

Bourbon Caramel Cookie Dough
with Toasted Walnuts & Marshmallows

SERVES 3

INGREDIENT

Bourbon Caramel
1 cup granulated sugar
¼ cup water
1 Tablespoon light corn
  syrup
½ cup heavy cream,
  warmed
¼ cup vanilla bourbon
2 Tablespoons butter

Cookie Dough
½ cup all-purpose flour
8 Tablespoons butter,
  room temperature
1/3 cup granulated
  sugar
1/3 cup caramel sauce
½ teaspoon granulated
  salt
3 Tablespoons milk
½ cup shelled walnuts,
  toasted and chopped
½ cup mini
  marshmallows

DIRECTIONS

Make caramel: In a large sauce pan, gently mix the sugar, water and corn syrup, being careful not to splatter the sugary liquid on the side of the pans. Use a clean pastry brush and cold water to wash down the inside of the pan if needed. Place the pan over medium heat. Do not stir!

Watch closely and allow the mixture to begin to caramelize. If you notice the center of the sugar becoming darker then the outer ring, gently swirl the sugar, but do no stir it. Cook until it is a medium to dark amber color. Remove from heat.

Slowly stir in the warmed cream. Then add the vanilla bourbon and finally the butter. Stir until well incorporated. Allow caramel to cool, mixing occasionally.

Make cookie dough: Preheat the oven to 350 degrees Fahrenheit. Prepare a pan with parchment or a Silpat and spread the flour onto the pan.

Bake for 5 minutes. Then allowing it to cool completely. Sift cooled flour and set aside.

In a stand mixer with a paddle attachment, mix the butter and sugar together.

Scrap down the bowl and add 1/3 cup cooled caramel sauce.

Scrape down the bowl again and add the salt and flour. Mix gently to incorporate.

Mix in milk and stir until smooth.

Finally add the walnuts and marshmallows and mix by hand. Serve immediately or store in an airtight container in the fridge for 3 days.

I was introduced to edible, raw cookie dough when I was in high school. The cafe that sold this decadent treat was a favorite stop for my group of friends. This is a twist on the classic flavors we enjoyed so much!

Red Velvet Cookie Bars

SERVES 16

INGREDIENT

2 large eggs
1 egg yolk
8 Tablespoons butter,
   melted and slightly
   cooled
1 box (15.25 ounce) red
   velvet cake mix
1 cup high-quality
   white chocolate chips

DIRECTIONS

Preheat oven to 350 degrees Fahrenheit. Prepare a 9"x 9" baking dish with non-stick baker's spray. Set aside.

In a large bowl lightly mix the eggs, yolk and butter together.

Stir the cake mix into the egg mixture.

Fold in the chocolate chips.

Press the cookie batter into the prepared pan as evenly as possible.

Bake for 27 minutes for softer bars or up to 30 minutes for more firm bars.

Cool and cut as desired. Use a heart cookie cutter for a little something extra special!

For Asher

Espresso Tour and Class
Florence, Italy

Making Muffins
Biloxi, Mississippi

Blending Milkshakes
Biloxi, Mississippi

Fish & Chips
London, England

Dessert Time!
Biloxi, Mississippi

Buying Chocolates
Brussels, Belgium

Fun After Cooking Class
Lucca, Italy

Birthday Cupcakes
Biloxi, Mississippi

Chef Paolo Monti
and "Baby Chef"
Lucca, Italy

Coffee Factory Tour
Florence, Italy

French Toast Breakfast
Biloxi, Mississippi

Disneyland Paris
Paris, France

125

Cake by the ocean
Corpus Christi, Texas

Making Pasta
Lucca, Italy

Baking with Mom
Schaumburg, Illinois

His First Apron
San Antonio, Texas

Gyros!
Mykonos, Greece

Caribbean Cruise
Galveston, Texas

First Time in the Kitchen
2 Months Old
Avane, Italy

First Birthday Cupcake
Livorno, Italy

Cutting Apples for a Strudel
Biloxi, Mississippi

Birthday Celebration
Avane, Italy

Our Little Chef
Avane, Italy

Christmas Cookies
San Antonio, Texas

Cooling Off with Lemon Ice
Venice, Italy

Cupcakes Near the Gulf
Fort Walton Beach, Florida

Hofbrauhaus Munchen
Munich, Germany

Our Wedding Cake
Disney's Boardwalk
Orlando, Florida

Italian Cooking Class
Lucca, Italy

Pastry School
Elgin, Illinois

"Meeting" Paula Deen
Savannah, Georgia

Magical Mickey Cookie
Orlando, Florida

Vineyard Tour
Pisa, Italy

About the Author

It might surprise a lot of people that I was a picky eater growing up. I lived on liverwurst sandwiches (*I know, it's a weird food for a kid to love*) and bologna sandwiches for much of my childhood. I didn't even like cake! But once I really began baking and cooking in high school I found a world I had completely missed.

After high school I attended a local pastry school and graduated with my Associate in Applied Science in Pastry Arts. Since then I have honed my skills baking for family, friends and many wonderful men and women of our military.

Beyond baking, I'm a proud mom of the most energetic, sweet and loving little boy - Asher. I'm also the wife of an accomplished Air Force Officer, Eric. Both of them, along with so many people we have met around the world have inspired these recipes. I've been incredibly blessed to have traveled extensively and have had so many once in a lifetime experiences that have shaped who I am today.

www.JennasDeliciousCreations.com
Instagram @MeasureAndPour

First Edition

Lightning Source UK Ltd.
Milton Keynes UK
UKHW051136100921
390301UK00005B/76